Gerald R. Ford

History Maker Bios

Laura Hamilton Waxman

⌐ LERNER PUBLICATIONS COMPANY • MINNEAPOLIS

Lerner Publications Company
A division of Lerner Publishing Group, Inc.
241 First Avenue North
Minneapolis, MN 55401 U.S.A.

Website address: www.lernerbooks.com

Library of Congress Cataloging-in-Publication Data

Waxman, Laura Hamilton.
    Gerald R. Ford / by Laura Hamilton Waxman.
       p.   cm. — (History maker biographies)
    Includes bibliographical references and index.
    ISBN 978–0–8225–7985–4 (lib. bdg. : alk. paper)
    1. Ford, Gerald R., 1913–2006—Juvenile literature. 2. Presidents—United
States—Biography—Juvenile literature. I. Title.
    E866.W395 2008
    973.925092—dc22 [B]   2007042189

Manufactured in the United States of America
1 2 3 4 5 6 – PA – 13 12 11 10 09 08

TABLE OF CONTENTS

INTRODUCTION

Gerald R. Ford was our nation's thirty-eighth president. But being president had not been his dream. As a young man, he wanted to be a U.S. lawmaker. His fairness, honesty, and outgoing personality gained him the voters' trust. Voters first elected him to the U.S. Congress in 1948. After that, they reelected him twelve more times.

In 1973, President Richard Nixon asked Ford to be his new vice president. About a year later, Nixon quit his job as president. He had been caught acting dishonestly and breaking the law. This scandal became known as Watergate. It angered many U.S. citizens.

Ford became the only U.S. president not elected as vice president or president. Even so, he worked hard to bring honor and honesty back to the White House. His fair and steady leadership helped the nation.

This is his story.

1 A TEAM PLAYER

Gerald R. Ford was born Leslie Lynch King Jr. on July 14, 1913. His mother, Dorothy Ayer Gardner, had married Leslie Lynch King Sr. They lived in Omaha, Nebraska. But young Leslie and his mother did not stay there long.

Leslie's mother and father divorced when he was a baby. He moved with his mother to his grandparents' home in Grand Rapids, Michigan.

Leslie's mother remarried when he was two years old. Her new husband, Gerald Rudolf Ford, was a paint salesman. Gerald loved Leslie as if he were his own son. He even gave the boy his name. Leslie became Gerald R. Ford Jr. His friends and family called him Jerry.

Jerry's new father took him fishing and played games with him. He also taught Jerry the importance of hard work and honesty. Dorothy Ford taught her son to treat people fairly and do the right thing.

When Jerry was born, his mother (RIGHT) nicknamed him Junie. The name was short for "Junior."

Jerry (SECOND FROM LEFT) poses with his half-brothers Tom (LEFT) and Dick (THIRD FROM LEFT). Jerry Ford Sr.holds baby Jim (FRONT).

The Fords were also strict with their children. They expected Jerry and his younger brothers to help with chores around the house. They also taught their sons to follow three family rules. "Tell the truth, work hard, and come to dinner on time."

At school, Jerry had a knack for getting along with almost anyone. He always tried to see the good in people. His classmates liked his positive and friendly attitude.

In his free time, Jerry loved to play sports. Football and baseball were two of his favorites. He played hard but fair.

In eighth grade, Jerry tried out for the school's football team. By high school, he had become one of his team's star players. Jerry loved the competition of the game. He also enjoyed being part of a team.

Jerry's father always told him, "The harder you work, the better your luck." Jerry took this advice to heart. At each game, he played his best. He inspired his teammates to do the same. He became a natural team leader.

MEETING LESLIE KING

Jerry met his birth father one day when he was sixteen years old. Leslie Lynch King drove a fancy car. He took Jerry to an expensive lunch. But he didn't seem interested in getting to know his son. At the end of the meal, King gave Jerry some money. Then he drove away. He never tried to visit his son again. That made Jerry sad. But he knew his true father would always be Gerald R. Ford Sr.

During his last year of high school, Jerry took a trip to Washington, D.C. He joined thirty other seniors from different cities in the Midwest. Jerry loved touring the nation's capital. He especially enjoyed visiting the House of Representatives. This group of 435 lawmakers makes up the lower branch of Congress. The Senate makes up the upper branch.

Jerry liked watching members of the House help create the nation's laws. He thought he might want to be a lawmaker in the House someday.

Grand Rapids' All City First Football Team 1930

During his senior year of high school, Jerry (BOTTOM CENTER) played center on the Grand Rapids All-City Football Team.

Jerry gets ready to play a game at Michigan Stadium.

Jerry graduated in 1931. He had grown into a tall, strong, confident young man. That fall, he entered the University of Michigan.

There, he played for the school's football team. Sometimes his team competed in front of one hundred thousand people. The fans put a lot of pressure on Jerry and the other players to win. But Jerry always stayed calm and steady.

Jerry finished college in 1935. Two professional football teams asked him to play for them. But Jerry turned them down. He had other plans. He wanted to study law and become a lawyer. After that, he hoped to follow his dream of becoming a lawmaker.

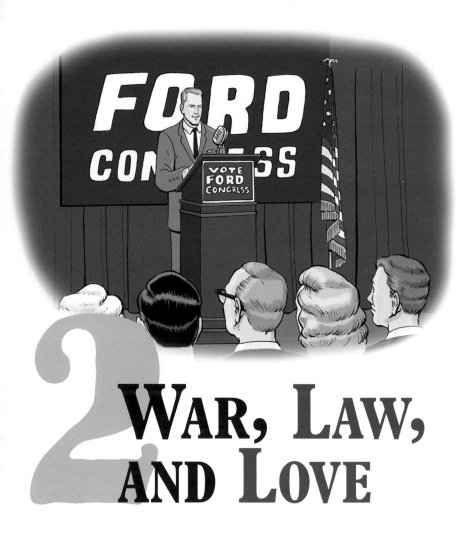

2 WAR, LAW, AND LOVE

Jerry Ford got his law degree at Yale
University in Connecticut. In 1941, he
returned home. He and a friend opened
their own law firm. They worked hard
and made their firm into a success. Then
everything changed.

In 1942, the United States entered World War II (1939–1945). This war had begun in Europe three years earlier. Ford wanted to help fight for his country. He joined the U.S. Navy right away.

By 1943, he was working on the USS *Monterey*. This ship carried U.S. fighter planes. Sometimes the ship itself was attacked by the enemy. Ford led the crew in gun battles. The men appreciated his steady, positive leadership.

Ford (LEFT) stands with fellow officer Truman Wallin on the deck of the USS MONTEREY in April 1944.

Ford returned home to Grand Rapids in 1946. His dream to be a lawmaker had grown stronger then ever. The war had taught him that good leaders were needed to keep world peace. The country also needed good leaders to help run the government.

Like many people in Grand Rapids, Ford's family belonged to the Republican Party. Ford was a Republican too. He wanted to run for the U.S. House of Representatives.

First, Ford had to win the Republican primary. The primary took place before the general election. In the primary election, Republicans voted for candidates to run against the Democratic Party's candidates.

Ford (RIGHT) visits with farmworkers on a campaign stop.

Ford set up his campaign headquarters in a recycled military building called a Quonset (KWAN-set) hut.

Ford needed to beat a Republican congressperson named Bartel J. Jonkman. Jonkman had been in the House for ten years. He was very popular with the voters. But Ford did not believe the man was trustworthy or honest. He believed Michigan deserved better.

No one thought Ford had a chance of winning the primary. He was only thirty-four years old. And he had no lawmaking experience. But he remembered his father's advice. Hard work brings good luck.

Ford met with local voters. He showed them that he cared about their problems. He promised to be fair and hardworking. One by one, he earned their trust. The primary took place on September 14, 1948. To everyone's surprise, Ford won.

He shared the good news with his girlfriend, Elizabeth Bloomer. Betty was lively, fun, and intelligent. She worked as a fashion expert at a department store. She had also been a model and a dancer. Over time, they had fallen in love.

Betty Bloomer was born in Chicago. Her family moved to Grand Rapids, Michigan, when she was very young.

After their wedding, Betty and Jerry Ford stand between their parents. They got married in Grand Rapids.

A month after the primary, Ford and Betty were married. Their wedding took place on October 15. Then he got back to work. He still had an election to win.

The general election happened less than three weeks after the wedding. Most people in Ford's part of Michigan voted for Republicans. So he easily won. At last, his dream was coming true.

Ford talks with a visitor to his office in Washington, D.C.

The Fords moved to Washington, D.C., in January 1949. From the start, he loved his new job. He liked learning everything he could about how laws were made. And he enjoyed working with the other House members. It was like being a part of a team.

Ford's work as a lawmaker kept him very busy. But in 1950, he made time to be a father too. Betty gave birth to their first child, Michael.

That same year, Ford ran for reelection. Again, he won easily. Still, he did not take his popularity for granted. Whenever he could, he went back to Michigan to meet with voters. Every two years, he received at least 60 percent of their votes.

COMMITTEE WORK

Both the House and Senate are broken into smaller groups called committees. Each committee works on different types of bills. One of the most powerful House committees is the Appropriations Committee. This group of lawmakers helps decide how the government will spend its money. In 1951, the chair, or head, of this committee asked Ford to join the Appropriations Committee. It was a great honor. Even better, the experience taught Ford much about how the country is run.

Michigan voters weren't the only ones who liked Ford. Other lawmakers came to trust him too. He had a reputation for hard work, honesty, and fairness. And his friendly personality made it easy for him to get along with both political parties.

Two friends he made in the House were Democrat John F. Kennedy and Republican Richard M. Nixon. Both men had dreams of being president. Ford admired them. But he did not share their dream. He liked being part of a team.

3 CHALLENGES AND SURPRISES

Ford's good reputation in Congress continued to grow. At home, his family grew just as quickly. By 1957, he and Betty had three more children. They were John, Steven, and Susan. They lived in a new house just outside Washington, D.C.

21

Ford was still very busy. But he also spent time with his children. On Saturdays, he often took them with him to his office. They roamed the halls of Congress and played while he worked. He also tried to spend each Sunday at home with his family. And he made sure to go to his children's games and other important events

Gerald and Betty Ford had three sons: John (LEFT), Steven (MIDDLE), and Michael (RIGHT). They had a daughter, Susan, in 1957, the year after this portrait was taken.

Ford loved his work in Congress as much as ever. But he was ready for a new challenge. He wanted to be Speaker of the House. For several years, this top job had gone to a Democrat. Democrats had more representatives in the House than Republicans. They got to choose the Speaker.

THE WARREN COMMISSION

In 1961, John F. Kennedy became U.S. president. A man named Lee Harvey Oswald assassinated, or killed, him on November 22, 1963. The new president, Lyndon B. Johnson, created the Warren Commission. He asked this group of seven leaders to learn all they could about Oswald and the assassination. Johnson chose only one House Republican to be on the commission. He wanted someone open minded and fair. He picked Gerald Ford.

The Senate minority leader raises Ford's hand after his election to the position of House minority leader. The rest of the House Republicans applaud the election results.

The top job open to Republicans was the minority leader. In 1965, the House Republicans chose Gerald Ford for the job.

As minority leader, Ford helped the Republicans pass their ideas into laws. To do that, he had to keep his party's lawmakers united as a team. He also needed to bring Democrats and Republicans together in agreement. His friendly and straightforward leadership style made him just right for the job.

In 1969, Ford's friend Richard Nixon became U.S. president. Ford was happy to have a Republican in the White House. But Nixon seemed to be a secretive president. Some lawmakers and voters distrusted him. Even so, Ford stayed loyal to his friend. He campaigned for Nixon's reelection throughout 1972.

Richard Nixon (CENTER) meets with Ford (RIGHT) and other representatives in 1971.

That June, Ford learned about a break-in at the Democratic National Committee (DNC) office. The DNC works to get Democratic candidates elected. That year, DNC headquarters were in the Watergate, a group of office buildings, apartments, and a hotel. Five men had been caught breaking into the DNC office. The men had plans to spy on the DNC. They committed a crime when they broke into the office. Their plans to spy were also against the law.

Four of the five men accused of breaking into the DNC office stand with their attorney (CENTER) after their trial.

The news shocked Ford, as it did other citizens. Some Americans thought the five men had been working for Nixon. But Nixon said that he and his staff had nothing to do with the break-in. Ford believed him. So did many voters. They reelected Nixon.

Then, in 1973, Nixon's vice president, Spiro Agnew, was discovered breaking the law. Agnew had cheated on his taxes. He had also used his power to gain money for himself. Nixon asked Agnew to resign, or quit his job. To replace Agnew, Nixon chose Gerald R. Ford.

Spiro Agnew gives a farewell speech to the nation after leaving his job as vice president.

Ford had never wanted that job. He liked working as a lawmaker. But the president and his country needed him. He agreed to take on this new challenge. On December 6, 1973, he became the vice president of the United States.

Ford waves to the people in the House chamber after taking the oath of office as vice president in 1973.

WASHINGTON POST reporters Bob Woodward (LEFT) and Carl Bernstein (RIGHT) uncovered Nixon's illegal actions.

The American people were glad to have a new vice president. But they were growing less happy with Nixon. They had been learning more about the Watergate break-in from their newspapers and television. Reporters said that people working for Nixon had organized the break-in.

Ford asked Nixon if he or his staff had anything to do with the break-in. Nixon said no. Ford continued to believe him. But Nixon had lied. He had tried to hide the truth. He and his staff had also spied and acted dishonestly in other ways. The break-in, spying, and lies became known as the Watergate scandal.

Both Ford and the American people were angered and saddened by the truth. They wanted to trust their president. But they had lost all trust in Nixon. Many Americans did not believe he should continue to lead the country. Congress held hearings to decide that question. In the summer of 1974, Nixon quit his job as president.

When a president quits or dies, the vice president takes over his job. Nixon quit on the morning of August 9. That same day, Ford became president.

4 THE PEOPLE'S MAN

Gerald R. Ford became president out of duty to his country. He had not wanted the power or attention of the presidency. He hoped only to serve the people of his nation.

"I am the people's man," he said in one of his first speeches. He promised "to serve all the people and do the best that I can for America."

Warren Burger (RIGHT), chief justice of the U.S. Supreme Court, swears in Ford as president. Betty Ford stands beside them.

Ford knew that many citizens wanted to trust their president again. From the start, he tried to lead the country in an open, truthful way.

The American people liked their new president. But Nixon's past behavior still angered them. They wanted Nixon to be judged in a court of law. Many people thought he should be punished.

Ford knew that Nixon's trial would last for several years. It would be in the news day after day. And day after day, citizens would dwell on the unpleasant past. Ford believed a long trial would be terrible for the country. He wanted to help Americans focus on the future instead. He knew of only one way to make that happen.

U.S. presidents have the power to pardon, or forgive, a person's crimes. A pardoned criminal is freed of a trial and punishment. Presidents usually use this power only in special cases. Ford planned to use it for Nixon. He hoped the country could then begin to recover.

Ford (BACK RIGHT) meets with economic advisers during his first month as president.

Ford announces that he will pardon Richard Nixon.

Many members of Ford's staff told him not to pardon Nixon. They said it would anger citizens. It would ruin Ford's popularity, they told him. But Ford did not care about being popular. "I know what the people are going to say," he said. "But this is the right thing to do."

On September 8, 1974, Ford announced his decision on television. Few people understood the reason for the pardon at the time. Both the Congress and the public were furious. But Ford never doubted his choice. He just kept moving forward. He had a lot more work to do.

Nixon had been reaching out to countries in Europe, Asia, and the Middle East. As president, Ford did the same.

One of the United States' most dangerous enemies was the Soviet Union. This group of fifteen republics, or states, was ruled by Russia until 1991. In November 1974, President Ford met with the Soviet's leader, Leonid Brezhnev.

Together they began work on a treaty, or agreement. Both leaders agreed to make fewer nuclear weapons. These bombs can destroy entire cities and kill millions of people. Ford hoped the agreement would help keep peace between the two nations.

Ford and Soviet leader Leonid Brezhnev (RIGHT) sign an agreement to limit the development of new nuclear weapons.

Five months later, Ford turned his attention to the Southeast Asian country of Vietnam. For many years, the South and North Vietnamese had been at war with each other. U.S. soldiers had been fighting alongside the South Vietnamese. Thousands of soldiers had lost their lives in the Vietnam War (1957–1975). Many Americans wanted the fighting to stop. In April 1975, Ford declared an end to U.S. fighting in the war.

At the end of the war in Vietnam, military helicopters took thousands of U.S. citizens and South Vietnamese supporters to safety.

ASSASSINATION ATTEMPTS

As president, Ford traveled all over the country. In September 1975, he visited California to meet voters and give speeches. Two women at two different events tried to assassinate him. One was Lynette "Squeaky" Fromme. The other was Sara Jane Moore. Ford was not hurt by these women. But he knew he could have been killed. Still, he never stopped traveling the country so people could get to know him.

At home, Ford faced other problems. The U.S. economy was doing poorly. Prices for many things were going up. People were buying less. That meant companies sold less and made less money. They couldn't afford to pay all their workers. That led to fewer jobs and more unemployed people.

Ford worked with the Congress to help solve these problems. Together they cut taxes for many citizens. Lower taxes gave people more money to spend. Companies did better. More workers found jobs.

But Ford did not think tax cuts alone were enough to help the economy. He also worried about the U.S. government's deficit. A deficit occurs when the government spends more money than it earns. Ford thought too many bills from Congress called for too much government spending. Often he vetoed, or blocked, those bills from becoming law. That angered many members of Congress. But Ford remained sure of his choices. He believed he was doing the best that he could for his country.

5 MOVING ON

Most presidents serve for four years before there's another election. Ford became president in the middle of Nixon's term. That meant he had to run for reelection only two years after becoming president. The next election took place in November 1976.

Ford speaks at his first debate with Democratic candidate Jimmy Carter (LEFT).

Many voters were still angry with Ford for pardoning Nixon. Others worried about whether he was really cut out to be president. They thought he did not have the experience or intelligence to do the job. Sometimes he seemed to stumble or make mistakes when he spoke.

Ford had to beat the Democratic candidate Jimmy Carter. Ford worked hard to prove that he was the better choice. But Carter received just enough votes to beat Ford in the election.

Losing the election made Ford feel sad. Still, he knew that dwelling on the past would do him no good. He began looking forward to a new future.

Ford had spent twenty-seven years in politics. For the first time, he and Betty enjoyed a quieter life. They bought homes in California and Colorado. Ford had time to play golf and relax.

In 1979, he published his autobiography. He called the book *A Time to Heal.* Two years later, he celebrated the openings of the Gerald R. Ford Presidential Library and Museum. Both buildings are in Michigan.

The library contains historical papers, photographs, videotapes, and other items. They deal with the years when Ford was a lawmaker and president. The museum features exhibits about Ford's life and work.

The Gerald R. Ford Presidential Library stands on the campus of the University of Michigan in Ann Arbor.

The Betty Ford Center

In 1982, the Fords attended the opening of
the Betty Ford Center. The center is in Rancho
Mirage, California. It helps people overcome
addictions to alcohol and drugs. Four years earlier,
Betty herself realized that she had these problems.
At the time, many people kept their addictions
a secret. Betty wanted to change that. She felt
proud of her recovery. Her husband did too.
Together they openly shared Betty's experiences.

Early on, Ford began holding
conferences at the library and museum.
At these gatherings, he helped lead
discussions about important U.S. and world
events. He also traveled across the country,
giving speeches. In his speeches, he shared
his experiences and opinions.

Over time, people gained more respect for Ford's leadership as president. Many came to agree with his decision to pardon Nixon. They believed it took great courage to make such an unpopular decision.

In 1999, Ford received two famous awards. The first was the Presidential Medal of Freedom. This is the highest award given to a nonmilitary U.S. citizen. The second award was the Congressional Gold Medal. Both awards honored Ford for his work as president.

By the 2000s, Ford was in his late eighties. He began to have serious health problems. But he still spoke out about his opinions on current events. He was especially saddened by the terrorist attack in New York City on September 11, 2001.

Ford died on December 26, 2006. He was ninety-three years old. Thousands of people came to his funeral. They mourned the loss of an honest, hardworking man. They were grateful for all he had done for his country.

TIMELINE

GERALD R. FORD
WAS BORN ON
JULY 14, 1913.

In the year . . .

1913   Ford moved to Grand Rapids, Michigan, with his mother.

1916   his name changed to Gerald R. Ford Jr. after his mother remarried.   Age 3

1931   he graduated from high school and entered the University of Michigan.   Age 17

1935   he graduated from the University of Michigan.

1941   he graduated with a law degree from Yale.

1942   he joined the navy.

1948   he married Betty on October 15. he was elected to Congress.   Age 35

1949   he became a congressman on January 3.

1965   he became the minority leader.

1973   he became vice president on December 6.

1974   he became president on August 9. he pardoned Nixon on September 8.   Age 61

1975   Ford declared an end to the country's part in the Vietnam War in April.

1976   he lost the election to Jimmy Carter.

1979   Ford published his autobiography, *A Time to Heal.*

1981   he celebrated the openings of the Gerald R. Ford Presidential Library and Museum.

1999   he was awarded the Presidential Medal of Freedom and the Congressional Gold Medal.   Age 86

2006   Gerald R. Ford died on December 26 at the age of ninety-three.

A Ford, Not a Lincoln

The night Gerald Ford became vice president, he gave a short speech. He said, "I am a Ford, not a Lincoln." These simple words became one of his most famous lines. They described the kind of president he went on to become.

Ford was making two kinds of comparisons in his speech. The first was with another president, Abraham Lincoln. Lincoln is considered to be one of our country's greatest leaders. He led the nation during the 1860s. During that time, he inspired many citizens with his powerful and carefully written speeches. In comparison, Ford spoke plainly and simply. His way of speaking matched his personality. He thought of himself as a regular guy. And he was proud to be that way.

The second comparison was between two kinds of cars. A Lincoln is considered an expensive, fancy car. A Ford is a more practical car. Ford knew that he was a practical leader too. He did not want a lot of power or attention. He just wanted to work hard and get things done.

Ford plays with his family dog, Liberty, in the Oval Office.

FURTHER READING

Anderson, Dale. *Watergate: Scandal inside the White House.* **Minneapolis: Compass Point Books, 2006.** The author uses photos and words to describe the events that led up to President Nixon's resignation and Gerald Ford's taking over as president.

Feldman, Ruth Tenzer. *How Congress Works: A Look at the Legislative Branch.* **Minneapolis: Lerner Publications Company, 2004.** Feldman explains how the House of Representatives and the Senate work.

Landau, Elaine. *Friendly Foes: A Look at Political Parties.* **Minneapolis: Lerner Publications Company, 2004.** This book explains what political parties are—especially the Republican and Democratic parties—and how they work.

Murray, Stuart. *Vietnam War.* **New York: DK Publishing, 2005.** A combination of photos and words helps readers understand the history of this deadly war.

Santow, Dan. *Elizabeth Bloomer Ford.* **New York: Children's Press, 2000.** This is a biography of Betty Ford.

WEBSITES

First Lady Biography: Betty Ford
http://www.firstladies.org/biographies/firstladies.aspx?biography=39 This Web page from the National First Ladies' Library includes fast facts and a short biography about Betty Ford.

Gerald R. Ford Presidential Library and Museum
http://www.ford.utexas.edu/ This official website includes detailed information about the thirty-eighth president, including a link to many photographs.

White House Kids
http://www.whitehouse.gov/kids/presidents/geraldford.html
This site, especially for kids, offers fast facts about President
Ford from the official White House website.

SELECT BIBLIOGRAPHY

Brinkley, Douglas. *Gerald R. Ford.* New York: Times Books,
　　2007.

Cannon, James. *Time and Chance: President Ford's
　　Appointment with History.* New York: Harper Collins, 1994.

Ford, Gerald R. *A Time to Heal: The Autobiography of
　　Gerald R. Ford.* New York: Harper & Row, 1979.

Gerald R. Ford Presidential Library and Museum. "Gerald R.
　　Ford Biography." http://www.fordlibrarymuseum.gov/grf/
　　fordbiop.asp (March 18, 2008).

Gerald R. Ford Presidential Library and Museum. "Timeline of
　　Gerald R. Ford's Life and Career." http://www.ford.utexas
　　.edu/grf/timeline.pdf (March 18, 2008).

Reeves, Richard. *A Ford, Not a Lincoln.* New York: Harcourt
　　Brace, 1975.

Smith, J. Y., and Lou Cannon. "Gerald R. Ford, 93, Dies; Led in
　　Watergate's Wake." *Washington Post,* December 27, 2006.

Washington Post Company. "The Watergate Story."
　　Washingtonpost.com. 2008. http://www.washingtonpost
　　.com/wp-srv/politics/special/watergate/index.html
　　#chapters (March 18, 2008).

INDEX

Acknowledgments

For photographs and artwork: Courtesy Gerald R. Ford Library, pp. 4, 7, 8, 10, 11, 13, 14, 15, 16, 17, 18, 22, 24, 25, 32, 33, 34, 40, 45; © Wally McNamee/CORBIS, p. 26; AP Photo, p. 27; © Bettmann/CORBIS, pp. 28, 29; White House Photograph Courtesy Gerald R. Ford Library, p. 35; © Dirck Halstead/Liaison/Getty Images, p. 36; AP Photo/John M. Galloway, p. 41.
Front & Back cover: Courtesy Gerald R. Ford Library.

For quoted material: pp. 8, 45, *Gerald R. Ford, A Time to Heal: The Autobiography of Gerald R. Ford* (New York: Harper & Row, 1979); pp. 9, 31, 34, James Cannon, *Time and Chance: President Ford's Appointment with History* (New York: HarperCollins, 1994).